3-17-14

HAVE YOU HEARD THE NESTING BIRD?

Words by Rita Gray

Pictures by Kenard Pak

Houghton Mifflin Harcourt • Boston New York

Mourning doves take their morning stroll.

coah, cooo, cooo, coooo

Woodpecker calls from a tree with a hole.

cuk-cuk-cuk-cuk-cuk

Starling sings from a metal pole.

whistle-ee-wee-tree

But have you heard the nesting bird?

"What bird? Where?"

"That robin, nesting up there."

Sparrow makes a simple jingle.

chiddik, chiddik

Swallow slides from under a shingle.

ha-ha-chit-chit-chit,
ha-ha-twitter-twit!

Crow calls out, "Come meet and mingle!"

caw! caw! caw! caw!

But have you heard the nesting bird?

"Not a single tweet or trill."

"This nesting bird is so still!"

Cardinal wears a pointy hat.

cheer-cheer-cheer-
purdy-purdy-purdy

Chickadee is an acrobat.

chick-a-dee-dee-dee

Catbird sounds like a hungry cat.

meow! meow!

But have you heard the nesting bird?

"It doesn't sing, not even a bit!"

"All it does is sit and sit."

Blue jay's shriek is as sharp as a drill.

jay! jay!   jay! jay!

Whip-poor-will has his favorite trill.

whip-poor-will   whip-poor-will

Wood thrush turns the twilight still.

ee-oh-lay   ee-oh-laaay

But have you heard the nesting bird?

"It hasn't sung a single song."

"This bird has been sitting for so long!"

Wait, what's that . . . ?

Tapping   Cracking

"Something made a little sound!"

Breaking   Shaking

"The bird is starting to move around!"

Ruffling   Shuffling

"The bird flew off with something blue."

Cheeping   Peeping

"Look! Another robin is coming too!"

"The baby birds are here!"

A Word with the Bird

Q. Why are you so quiet in your nest?

A. *Incubating a clutch of eggs is quiet work. I don't want other animals to know I am hiding eggs. They might eat them!*

Q. Why do you spend almost all your time in your nest?

A. *My eggs depend on me for warmth and shade. If they get too hot or too cold, they will not survive. And a hard rain could wash them away! I also turn my eggs daily so that my babies do not stick to the inside of their shells.*

Q. How do you keep your eggs at the right temperature?

A. *I have a special place on my belly called a brood patch. It is a bald patch that lets my warmth go directly to the eggs. But when I feel my eggs getting too warm, I move away to give them some air. Later on, my feathers will grow back in. Otherwise, I would freeze in winter!*

Q. Do you ever leave the nest?

A. *Yes, for short periods of time, to eat and drink. But when it's cold or rainy, or very hot, I am needed there almost full-time.*

Q. Why did you fly off with something blue?

A. *That was a piece of broken eggshell. I remove all the broken shells to keep our nest clean. Also, the cracked shells would tell predators that my babies have hatched, so it's best to hide them far from our nest.*

Q. Where is the father bird?

A. *He's always nearby, protecting me and our territory. Sometimes he brings me food. Once the babies arrive, we take turns feeding them.*

Q. After the babies hatch, can they keep themselves warm and cool?

A. *Oh, no! The babies in our brood are practically naked and still need our protection.*

Q. What should I do if I find a bird sitting in her nest?

A. *Quietly watch her for a short period of time before moving away. Mother birds are uncomfortable when people stay near their nests, and they won't feel free to take their breaks.*

Q. Do birds live in nests all the time?

A. *No, we only use nests to raise our young. Once the babies can fly, they leave the nest forever.*

Q. But what happens to the babies after they leave the nest?

A. *We continue to care for our fledglings until they are ready to be on their own. So if you find a fully feathered fledgling on the ground, please leave it there. It might look alone, but it isn't.*

Q. Do you have a song?

A. *I make lots of different sounds to communicate, but mostly the father bird does the singing. In fact, that's why I picked him. I love his song! It goes like this:*

cheerily, cheer up!   my tree makes syrup!   syrup so sweet!

Well, that's what it sounds like to me, but you can make up your own words to birds' songs. Try it—it's fun!

For Andrea —R.G.

For my dear, graceful mother —K.P.

Special thanks to Marc Devokaitis at the Cornell Lab of Ornithology for reviewing the accuracy of the bird facts. Thanks also to Jeff Hoagland at the Stony Brook-Millstone Watershed Association for clarifying the correct relationship between nesting birds, new fledglings, and curious people.

www.hmhbooks.com

The text of this book is set in Hightower and Pencil Pete.
The art is watercolor and digital media.

Library of Congress Cataloging-in-Publication Data
Gray, Rita, author.
Have you heard the nesting bird? / by Rita Gray ; illustrated by Kenard Pak.
pp. cm.
Summary: "In this nonfiction picture book for young readers, we learn just why the mother nesting bird stays quiet and still while sitting on her eggs." — Provided by publisher.
Audience: Age 4 and up. Audience: Grades K to 3. ISBN 978-0-544-10580-5
1. Birds—Behavior—Juvenile literature. 2. Birds—Nests—Juvenile literature. 3. Birdsongs—Juvenile literature. I. Pak, Kenard, illustrator. II. Title.
QL698.3.G73 2014
598.156'4—dc23
2013017621

Manufactured in China
SCP 10 9 8 7 6 5 4 3 2 1

4500449961

To hear more robin songs and sounds, go to
www.learner.org/jnorth/tm/robin/Dictionary.html.